LEARN T...
SPEAK AND WRITE
JAPANESE

Other Books on
LANGUAGE

1. Learn to Speak and Write Arabic with CD (New)	195/-
2. Teach Yourself Spanish (With CD)	195/-
3. Learn to Speak and Write Russian with CD (New)	195/-
4. Learn to Speak and Write Korean with CD (New)	195/-
5. French Made Easy with CD (New)	150/-
6. Learn to Speak and Write French	110/-
7. Conversational Chinese	175/-
8. Learn to Speak and Write Italian	110/-
9. Learn to Speak and Write German	110/-
10. Learn to Speak and Write Spanish	110/-
11. Learn to Speak and Write Japanese	110/-
12. Learn to Speak and Write Hindi	125/-

lotus PRESS

Unit No. 220, Second Floor, 4735/22,
Prakash Deep Building, Ansari Road, Darya Ganj,
New Delhi - 110002, Ph.: 32903912, 23280047, 09811594448
E-mail: lotuspress1984@gmail.com, www.lotuspress.co.in

LEARN TO SPEAK AND WRITE JAPANESE

Deepak Katyal

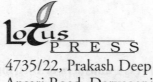

4735/22, Prakash Deep Building,
Ansari Road, Daryaganj,
New Delhi - 110002

Lotus Press Publishers & Distributors
Unit No.220, 2nd Floor, 4735/22, Prakash Deep Building,
Ansari Road, Daryaganj, New Delhi- 110002
Ph:- 32903912, 23280047, 098118-38000
Email : lotuspress1984@gmail.com
Visit us : www.lotuspress.co.in

Learn to Speak & Write Japanese
© 2015, Deepak Katyal
ISBN : 978-81-89093-86-0

Published by : **Lotus Press Publishers & Distributors,** New Delhi- 2
Printed at : **Bharat Offset Works,** New Delhi

Introduction To The Book...

Our books on **FOREIGN LANGUAGES** have been designed keeping in mind the increasing number of tourists, businessmen and others who visit these countries very often.

These books can also serve as a basis for a complete study of these languages.

Learners who use these books can easily make themselves understood where these languages are spoken. By reading these books, one is not required to learn a long list of grammatical rules.

The vocabularies in these books have been carefully selected to give every learner the words that are needed in all aspects of everyday life.

We, at Lotus Press, are pretty confident that these books will give the learners a useful introduction to these languages as they are spoken and written. This can eventually lead the learners to achieve a complete mastery on their chosen language.

LEARN TO SPEAK AND WRITE **JAPANESE** helps you to get acquainted with the Japanese language. This will surely enable you to speak and write Japanese as fluently just the way the typical Japanese do. Happy learning ...

– Publishers ◆

◆ TABLE OF CONTENTS ◆

Lesson 1

An insight of Japanese Language

Japan has a population of over 120 million, and linguistically, it is a nearly homogenous nation, with more than 99% of the population using the same language. This means that the Japanese language is the sixth most spoken language in the world. However, the language is spoken in scarcely any region outside Japan.

There are many theories about the origin of the Japanese language. A number of scholars believe that syntactically it is close to such Altaic languages as Turkish and Mongolian, and its syntactic similarity to Korean is widely acknowledged. There is also evidence that its morphology and vocabulary were influenced prehistorically by the Malayo-Polynesian languages to the south.

The Japanese writing system comes from Chinese, although the languages spoken by the Japanese and

Chinese are completely different. After Chinese writing was introduced sometime in the fifth or sixth century it was supplemented by 2 phonetic scripts that were transformed from the Chinese characters, *hiragana* and *katakana*.

A large number of local dialects are still used. Whereas standard Japanese, which is based on the speech of Tokyo, has been gradually spreading throughout the country under the influence of media such as radio, television and movies, the dialects spoken by the people of Kyoto and Osaka, in particular, continue to flourish and maintain their prestige.

Phonology

Speakers of Spanish and Italian will find that the short vowels of Japanese- *a, i, u, e, o* - are pronounced very similarly to the vowels of those languages. Long vowels - *aa, ii, uu, ei or ee, oo* - are produced by doubling the length of the short vowels (although *ei* is often pronounced as 2 separate vowels). The distinction between short and long vowels is crucial, as it changes the meaning of a word.

The consonants are *k, s, sh, t, ch, ts, n, h,f, m, y, r, w, g, j, z, d, b,* and *p*. The fricative *sh* (as in English *"shoot")*, along with the affricates *ch, ts,* and *j* (as in English *"charge," "gutsy",* and *"jerk"*, respectively) are treated as single consonants. The *g* sound is always the hard *g* of English *"game"*, not that of *"gene"*.

A major difference from English is that Japanese has no stress accent: equal stress is given each syllable. And whereas English syllables are sometimes elongated, in

Japanese, strings of syllables are spoken with the regularity of a metronome. Like English, Japanese does have a system of high and low pitch accents.

Grammar

As for basic structure, the typical Japanese sentence follows a pattern of subject-object-verb. For example, *Taro ga ringo o tabeta* literally means "Taro an apple ate."

Japanese often omit the subject or the object - or even both - when they feel that it will be understood from the context, that is, when the speaker or writer is confident that the person being addressed already has certain information about the situation in question. In such a case, the sentence given above might become, *ringo o tabeta* ("ate an apple") or simply *tabeta* ("ate").

In Japanese, unlike English, word order does not indicate the grammatical function of nouns in a sentence. Nor are nouns inflected for grammar case, as in some languages. Grammatical function is instead indicated by particles that follow the noun, the more important ones being *ga, wa, o, ni,* and *no.* The particle *wa* is especially important, because it flags the topic or theme of a sentence.

There is no indication of either person or number in Japanese verbal inflections. In the modern language, all verbs in their dictionary forms end in the vowel *u.* Thus in English it would be said that the verb *taberu* means "to eat," although actually it is the present tense and means "eat/eats" or "will eat." Some other inflectional forms are *tabenai* ("does not eat" or "will not eat"), *tabeyo* ("let's eat" or "someone may eat"), *tabetai* ("want/wants to eat"), *tabeta* ("ate"), *tabereba* ("if someone eats"), and *tabero* ("eat!").

Written Japanese

While the Chinese use their characters or ideograms to write each and every word, the Japanese devised 2 separate forms of phonetic script, called *kana,* to use in combination with Chinese characters. At times the written language also contains roman letters - in acronyms such as IBM, product numbers, and even entire foreign words - so that a total of 4 different scripts are needed to write modern Japanese.

Chinese characters - called *kanji* in Japanese - are actually ideograms, each one of which symbolises a thing or an idea. It is common for 1 *kanji* to have more than 1 sound. In Japan, they are used to write both words of Chinese origin and native Japanese words.

There are 2 forms of syllabic *kana* script. One is called *hiragana,* which was mainly used by women in the olden times. It consists of 48 characters and is used for writing native Japanese words, particles, verb endings, and often for writing those Chinese loan-words that cannot be written with the characters officially approved for general use.

The other *kana* script, called *katakana,* is also a group of 48 characters. It is chiefly used for writing loan-words other than Chinese, emphasising words, for onomatopoeia, and for the scientific names of flora and fauna.

Both kinds of *kana* are easier to write than the full forms of the original Chinese forms from which they were taken.

Although the more complete Japanese dictionaries carry definitions of up to 50,000 characters, the number currently in use is much smaller. In 1946, the Ministry of Education fixed the number of characters for general and official use at 1,850, including 996 taught at elementary and junior high school. This list was replaced in 1981 by a somewhat expanded though similar list of 1,945. Publications other than newspapers are not limited to this list, however, and many readers know the meaning of considerably more characters than are taught in the standard public school curriculum.

It is customary for Japanese to be written or printed in vertical lines that are read from top to bottom. The lines begin at the right-hand side of the page, and so ordinary books usually open from what would be the back of a Western-language book. Exceptions are books and periodicals devoted to special subjects - scientific and technical matter - which are printed in horizontal lines and read from left to right. Nowadays there is a tendency to print books in horizontal lines. These publications open in the same way as their Western counterparts.

Loan-Words

Japanese has not only an abundance of native words but also a large number of words whose origin is Chinese. Many of the Chinese loan-words are today so much a part of daily language that they are not perceived to have come from outside Japan. The cultural influence of China over the centuries was such that many words used in an intellectual or philosophical context are of Chinese origin. When new concepts were introduced from the West during the late nineteenth and early twentieth century, they were often translated by making up new combinations of Chinese characters, and such words represent a significant body of intellectual vocabulary used by modern Japanese.

To these loan-words are added many words borrowed from English and other European languages. While this coining of new words continues, it has been common to use Western words as they are, for example, "volunteer," "newscaster" and so on. Japanese also invented such pseudo-English words as "nighter" for night games and "salaryman" for the salaried worker. This tendency has markedly increased in recent years.

Honorific Language

The Japanese have developed an entire system of honorific language, called *keigo,* that is used to show a speaker's respect for the person being spoken to. This involves different levels of speech, and the proficient user of *keigo* has a wide range of words and expressions from which to choose, in order to produce just the desired degree of politeness. A simple sentence could be expressed in more than 20 different ways depending on the status of the speaker relative to the person being addressed.

Deciding on an appropriate level of polite speech can be quite challenging, since relative status is determined by a complex combination of factors, such as social status, rank, age, gender, even favours done or owed. There is a neutral or middle-ground level of language that is used when 2 people meet for the first time, are not aware of each other's group affiliation, and whose social standing appears to be similar (that is, no obvious differences in dress or manner). In general, women tend to speak a more polite style of language than men, and to use it in a broader range of circumstances.

Mastery of *keigo* is by no means simple, and some Japanese are much more proficient in it than others. The almost countless honorific terms are found in various parts of speech-nouns, adjectives, verbs, and adverbs. So-called exalted terms are used when referring to the addressee and things directly associated with him or her, such as relatives, the house, or possessions. By contrast, there are special humble terms that one uses as the speaker, when referring to oneself or things associated with oneself. It is the distance created by these 2 contrasting modes that expresses the proper attitude of respect for the person being spoken to.

Names

Japanese have family names and given names, used in that order. (English-language newspapers and magazines in Japan, however, usually present names in the order common among Western cultures, with given name first.) When addressing another person it is common to use *san* - the equivalent of Mr., Mrs. (or Ms.) - after the family name.

The suffix *chan* is often attached to children's names and given names of close friends. Other titles, such as *sensei* for "teacher" or "doctor," are also attached as suffixes after the family name.

Given names and their Chinese characters are chosen for their auspicious meanings and happy associations in the hope that they will bring the child good luck. The government has authorised a total of 2,229 characters to be used as given names.

Lesson 2

The Japanese Alphabet

Japanese has two kinds of alphabet, Hiragana and Katakana. Hiragana is used when we have no Japanese characters (*Kanji*) for the words or we don't remember the right Kanji. Katakana is used mainly for foreign names.

Basically, Japanese has only five vowels, a, i, u, e, o. In connection with consonants, k, s, t, n, h (*or f*) m, y, we have 48 alphabets.

Hiragana

a	i	u	e	o
ka	ki	ku	ke	ko
sa	shi	su	se	so
ta	chi	tsu	te	to
na	ni	nu	ne	no
ha	hi	hu	he	ho
ma	mi	mu	me	mo

Katakana

a	i	u	e	o
ka	ki	ku	ke	ko
sa	shi	su	se	so
ta	chi	tsu	te	to
na	ni	nu	ne	no
ha	hi	hu	he	ho
ma	mi	mu	me	mo

Learn to Speak and Write JAPANESE

ya	yu	yo				ya	yu	yo		
ra	ri	ru	re	ro		ra	ri	ru	re	ro
wq	wo					wq	wo			
nn						nn				

Lesson 3

Pronunciation

Japanese is not a difficult language to learn, of course, it is a little hard to master all Japanese writing, but for speaking it is not as hard as you think.

Here are some facts.

Japanese is easy to pronounce. It has only five vowels.

Japanese nouns do not have gender, and rarely, number aspects. With most Japanese nouns, number is not an issue. The same word is used for one or more than one.

Vowels

The Japanese language has only 5 vowels: A, I, U, E, O. They are terse vowels, pronounced clearly and sharply. If one pronounces the vowels in the following sentence one will have their approximate sounds. Please note: the "U" is pronounced with no forward movement of the lips. There are five general (*root*) sounds to pronunciation. These are:

Sound	Example
A	Ta(*da*), ...
I	(*The letter*) E, chief, (*Spanish word*) si
U	you, to, true
E	Thames (river), fetch, net
O	No, pole, profession, ... (*cut these sounds short*)

Long vowel syllables

Each of the long syllables is pronounced by simply extending the short vowel. Here are examples.

aa

e.g. mother okaasan

ii

e.g. good ii

uu

e.g. air kuuki

ee

e.g. movie eega

oo

e.g. big ookii

n

Syllabic consonants n is pronounced as follows.

Before the consonants n, t and d, it is pronounced "n" as in "night".

e.g. problem mondai

Before the consonants m, p and b, it is pronounced "m' S as in "moon'.

e.g. pencil enpitsu

Before the consonants k, g and ng, it is pronounced "ng" as in "sing".

e.g. music ongaku

Before the vowels and other consonants not mentioned above, it is pronounced as a nasal vowel.

e.g. teacher sensei

Double consonants pp, tt, ss, kk

pp

It is similar to the "p" sound in the English word "shopping".

e.g. one minute ippun

tt

It is similar to the "t" sound in the English word "cutter".

e.g. stamp kitte

ss

It is similar to the "s" sound in the English word "dressing".

e.g. straight massugu

kk

It is similar to the "k" sound in the English word "booking".

e.g. the forth day of the month **yokka**

Lesson 4

Numbers in Japanese

There are several differences between the way Japanese and Indo-European languages deal with numbers. First of all, in Japanese there are two words for four, seven, and nine, but they're not interchangeable; you just have to know which one to use in each case. For instance, when counting, you say shi for four, but in phone numbers, you say yon. When referring to the month of April, which is said literally as "4-month", you again use shi. (*For seven, the two words are shichi and nana, and for nine they are ku and kyu*).

But that's only the beginning of the number woes. When referring to numbers of particular objects, there are two systems. One uses a number word, like those mentioned in the above paragraph, plus a "counter," which indicates what type of object you are talking about. The other system has completely different number words, but forgoes the need for a counter.

The numbers from one to ten are pronounced as follows:

one ichi

two ni

three san

four shi

five go

six roku

seven shichi

eight hachi

nine kyu

ten ju

Above ten the numbers are pronounced differently: for example the number 11 in Japanese is translated as "10 plus 1"

eleven ju ichi

twelve ju ni

thirteen ju san

fourteen ju shi

fifteen ju go

sixteen ju roku

seventeen ju shichi

eighteen ju hachi

nineteen ju kyu

Above the number twenty the numbers are again pronounced in a slightly different manner. For example the number 20 in Japanese translates as "2 - 10's" and continuing on therefore, the number 21 would be considered as "2 - 10's plus 1"

twenty ni ju

twenty-one ni juichi

twenty-two ni juni

and so on - all the way up to the number 99.

For example the number 56 would be "5 - 10's plus 6" - or - "gojuroku" - the number 61 would then be "6 - 10's plus 1" - or - "rokujuichi" and so on and so on.

The number 100 is pronounced as "hyaku" so counting above 100 is basically just a matter of adding the word "hyaku" in the appropriate place and then following the same general principle for example the number 150 is pronounced as "hyakugoju".

Now here are the Japanese counter for objects learn this well!

1.	*hitotsu*
2.	*futatsu*
3.	*mittsu*
4.	*yottsu*
5.	*itsutsu*
6.	*muttsu*
7.	*nanatsu*

8.	*yatsu*
9.	*kokonotsu*
10.	*tou*

then continue counting with regular numbers as in regular numbers.

How many *ikutsu*

Counting people

here we use the suffix *"nin"* but this changes depending on the number before and 1 and 2 have exceptions again just learn by counting over and over out loud.

1.	person *hitori*
2.	people *futari*
3.	people *sannin*
4.	people *yonin*
5.	people *gonin*
6.	people *rokunin*
7.	people *shichinin*
8.	people *hachinin*
9.	people *kunin*
10.	people *junin*

How many people *nannin*

Counting flat things

Example: Paper, plates etc. uses suffix *"mai"*

1.	*ichimai*
2.	*nimai*
3.	*sanmai*
4.	*yonmai*

5. **gomai**
6. **rokumai**
7. **nanamai**
8. **hachimai**
9. **kyumai**
10. **jumai**

How many **nanmai**

Counting long slender things

The counter here is suffix **"hon"**.

Example: Pencils, sticks, etc..

1. **ippon**
2. **nihon**
3. **sanbon**
4. **yohon**
5. **gohon**
6. **roppon**
7. **nanahon**
8. **happon**
9. **kyuhon**
10. **jyuppon**

How many **nanbon**

Counting books

The Counter here is **"satsu"**.

1. Book   **issatsu**
2. Books   **nisatsu**
3. Books   **sansatsu**
4. Books   **yonsatsu**

5.	Books	**gosatsu**
6.	Books	**rokusatsu**
7.	Books	**nanasatsu**
8.	Books	**hassatsu**
9.	Books	**kyusatsu**
10.	Books	**jissatsu**

How many **nansastu**

Lesson 5

Nouns

Japanese nouns are non-inflecting, have no gender, and take no articles. Thus *neko* could be translated into English as "cat", "a cat", "the cat", "cats", "some cats", or "the cats", depending on context. A small number of nouns have plurals formed by reduplication (*possibly accompanied by rendaku*): thus *hito* "person" and *hitobito* "people", although these are typically collective rather than true plurals. Additionally, in respectful speech, the prefix *o-* is often used with native nouns, as is the prefix *go-* with Sino-Japanese nouns. Some common nouns have unpredictable respectful forms; a few examples are in the adjoining table.

meaning	plain	respectful
rice	*meshi*	*go-han*
money	*kane*	*o-kane*
body	*karada*	*o-karada*
		onmi

Lesson 6

Verbs

One of the characteristics of the Japanese language is that the verb generally comes at the end of the sentence. Since Japanese's sentences often omit the subject, the verb is probably the most important part in understanding the sentence. However, Verbs forms are considered to be difficult to learn. The good news is the system itself is rather simple, as far as memorizing certain rules. Unlike the more complex verb conjugation of other languages, Japanese verbs do not have a different form to indicate the person (*first-, second-, and third-person*), the number (*singular and plural*), or gender.

Japanese verbs are roughly divided into three groups according to their dictionary form (*basic form*).

U ending Verbs

The basic form of Group 1 verbs end with "~ u". This group is also called Consonant-stem verbs or Godandoushi (*Godan verbs*).

Group 1 Verbs

hanasu	to speak
kaku	to write
kiku	to listen
matsu	to wait
nomu	to drink

Iru and Eru ending Verbs

The basic form of Group 2 verbs end with either "~iru"
or "~ eru". This group is also called Vowel-stem-verbs or
Ichidan-doushi (*Ichidan verbs*).

Group 2 Verbs

~ **iru** ending	**kiru**	to wear
	miru	to see
	okiru	to get up
	oriru	to get off
	shinjiru	to believe
~ **eru** ending	**akeru**	to open
	ageru	to give
	deru	to go out
	neru	to sleep
	taberu	to eat

There are some exceptions. The following verbs belong
to Group 1, though they end with "~ iru" or "~ eru".

hairu	to enter
hashiru	to run
iru	to need
kaeru	to return
kagiru	to limit

kiru	to cut
shaberu	to chatter
shiru	to know

Irregular Verbs

There are only two irregular verbs, **kuru** (*to come*) and **suru** (*to do*).

The verb "suru" is probably the most often used verb in Japanese. It is used as "to do," "to make," or "to cost". It is also combined with many nouns (*of Chinese or Western origin*) to make them into verbs. Here are some examples.

benkyousuru	to study
ryokousuru	to travel
yushutsusuru	to export
dansusuru	to dance
shanpuusuru	to shampoo

Lesson 7

The Verb Conjugation

Dictionary Form

The dictionary form (*basic form*) of all Japanese verbs end with "u". This is the form listed in the dictionary, and is the informal, present affirmative form of the verb. This form is used among close friends and family in informal situations.

The ~ masu Form (Formal Form)

The suffix "~ masu" is added to the dictionary form of the verbs to make sentence polite. Aside from changing the tone, it has no meaning. This form is used in situations required politeness or a degree of formality, and is more appropriate for general use.

The ~ masu Form

Group 1   Take off the final ~u, and add ~ **imasu**
                 **kaku — kakimasu, nomu —
                 nomimasu**

Group 2	Take off the final **~ru**, and add **~masu** — miru — **mimasu**, taberu — **tabemasu**
Group 3	**kuru** — **kimasu**, **suru** — **shimasu**

The ~ masu Form minus "~ masu" is the stem of the verb. The verb stems are useful since many verb suffixes are attached to them.

~ Masu Form	The stem of the verb
kakimasu	**kaki**
nomimasu	**nomi**
mimasu	**mi**
tabemasu	**tabe**

Present Tense

Japanese verb forms have two main tenses, the present and the past. There is no future tense. The present tense is used for future and habitual action as well. The informal form of the present tense is the same as the dictionary form. The ~ masu form is used in formal situations.

Past Tense

The past tense is used to express actions completed in the past (*I saw, I bought etc.*) and present perfect tense (*I have read, I have done etc.*). Forming the informal past tense is simpler for Group 2 verbs, but more complicated for Group 1 verbs. The conjugation of Group 1 verbs varies depending on the consonant of the last syllable on the dictionary form. All Group 2 verbs have the same conjugation pattern.

Group 1

Formal	Replace ~ **u** with ~ **imashita**	**kaku — kakimashita nomu — nomimashita**
Informal	(1) Verb ending with ~ **ku**: replace ~ **ku** with ~ **ita**	**kaku — kaita kiku — kiita**
	(2) Verb ending with ~ **gu**: replace ~ **gu** with ~ **ida**	**isogu — isoida oyogu — oyoida**
	(3) Verb ending with ~ **u**, ~**tsu** and ~ **ru**: replace them with ~ **tta**	**utau — utatta matsu — matta kaeru — kaetta**
	(4) Verb ending with ~ **nu**, ~**bu** replace them with ~ **nda** and ~ **mu**:	**shinu — shinda asobu — asonda nomu — nonda**
	(5) Verb ending with ~ **su**: replace ~ **su** with ~ **shita**	**hanasu — hanashita dasu — dashita**

Group 2

Formal	Take off ~**ru**, and add ~ **mashita**	**miru — mimashita taberu —tabemashita**
Informal	Take off ~**ru**, and add ~ **ta**	**miru — mita taberu — tabeta**

Group 3

Formal	**kuru — kimashita, suru — shimashita**
Informal	**kuru — kita, suru —shita**

Present Negative

To make sentence negative, verb endings are changed into negative forms (*The ~ nai Form*).

Formal   All Verbs (Group 1, 2, 3)

Replace ~ **masu**   **nomimasu —**
with ~ **masen**   **nomimasen**
                             tabemasu —
                             tabemasen
                             kimasu —
                             kimasen
                             shimasu —
                             shimasen

Group 1

Informal

Replace the final   **kiku — kikanai**
~ **u** with ~**anai**   **nomu —**
(If verb ending is a   **nomanai**
vowel + ~ u,   **au — awanai**
replace with ~ **wanai**)

Group 2

Repl ~ ~ **ru** with ~ **nai**   **miru — minai**
                                   taberu — tabenai

Group 3

kuru — konai, suru —shinai

Past Negative

Formal   All Verbs (Group 1, 2, 3)

    Add ~ **deshita** to
the formal present
negative form

nomimasen —
nomimasen
deshita
tabemasen —
tabemasen
deshita
kimasen —
kimasen deshita
shimasen —
shimasen deshita

Informal   All Verbs (Group 1, 2, 3)

    Replace ~ **nai**
with ~ **nakatta**

nomanai —
nomanakatta
tabenai —
tabenakatta
konai —
konakatta
shinai —
shinakatta

Lesson 8

The ~ te form

The ~ te form is a useful form of the Japanese verb. It does not indicate tense by itself, however it combines with other verb forms to create other tenses. It has many other uses as well. To make the ~ te form, replace the final ~ ta of the informal past tense of the verb with ~ te, and ~ da with ~ de.

Informal Past	The ~ te form
nonda	**nonde**
tabeta	**tabete**
kita	**kite**

Here are some other functions of the ~ te form.

(1) Request: the ~ te form + kudasai

Mite kudasai.	Please look.
Kiite kudasai.	Please listen.

(2) The present progressive: the ~ te form + iru or imasu (formal)

Hirugohan o tabete iru.	I am having lunch.

Terebi o mite imasu.   I am watching TV.

It is also used to describe a habitual action and a condition.

(3) Listing successive actions

It is used to connect two or more verbs. The ~ te form is used after all but the last sentence in a sequence.

Hachi-ji ni okite gakkou ni itta.   I got up at eight and went to school.

Depaato ni itte kutsu o katta.   I went to department store and bought shoes.

(4) Asking permission: the ~ te form + mo ii desu ka.

Terebi o mite mo ii desu ka.   May I watch TV?

Tabako o sutte mo ii desu ka.   May I smoke?

Lesson 9

The Adjectives

There are two types of adjectives in Japanese: **i-adjectives** and **na-adjectives**. I-adjectives all end in "~ i," though they never end in "~ ei" (*e.g. "kirei" is not an i-adjective*)

Japanese adjectives differ from their English counterparts. Although Japanese adjectives have functions to modify nouns like English adjectives, they also function as verbs when used as predicates. For example, "takai" in the sentence "takai kuruma" means, "expensive". "Takai" of "kono kuruma wa takai" means not just "expensive" but "is expensive". When i-adjectives are used as predicates, they may be followed by "~ desu" to indicate a formal style. "Takai desu" also means, "is expensive" but it is more formal than "takai".

Here are lists of common i-adjectives and na-adjectives.

Common I-Adjectives

atarashii	new	**furui**	old
atatakai	warm	**suzushii**	cool
atsui	hot	**samui**	cold
oishii	delicious	**mazui**	bad tasting
ookii	big	**chiisai**	small
osoi	late, slow	**hayai**	early, quick
omoshiroi	interesting, boring	**tsumara--nai**	funny
kurai	dark	**akarui**	bright
chikai	near	**tooi**	far
nagai	long	**mijikai**	short
muzukashii	difficult	**yasashii**	easy
ii	good	**warui**	bad
takai	tall, high	**hikui**	low
yasui	cheap	**wakai**	young
isogashii	busy	**urusai**	noisy

Common Na-Adjectives

ijiwaruna	mean	**shinsetsuna**	kind
kiraina	distasteful	**sukina**	favourite
shizukana	quiet	**nigiyakana**	lively
kikenna	dangerous	**anzenna**	safe
benrina	convenient	**fubenna**	inconve--nient

kireina	pretty	**genkina**	healthy, -well
jouzuna	skillful	**yuumeina**	famous
teineina	polite	**shoujikina**	honest
gankona	stubborn	**hadena**	showy

Lesson 10

The use of Adjectives

When used as modifiers of nouns, both i-adjectives and na-adjectives take the basic form, and precede nouns just like in English.

I-Adjectives	**chiisai inu**	small dog
	takai tokei	expensive watch
Na-Adjectives	**yuumeina gaka**	famous painter
	sukina eiga	favourite movie

I-Adjectives as Predicates

As mentioned on the previous page, adjectives can function like verbs. Therefore, they conjugate just like verbs (*but probably much more simply*).

Informal	Present Negative	Replace the final ~ **i** with ~ **ku nai**
	Past	Replace the final ~ **i** with ~ **katta**

	Past Negative	Replace the final ~ **i** with ~ **ku nakatta**

Add ~**desu** to all of the informal forms.

Formal — There is also a variation in the formal negative forms.
* Negative: Replace ~**i** with ~**ku arimasen**
* Past Negative: Add ~ **deshita** to ~**ku arimasen**
These negative forms are considered slightly more polite than others.

Here is how the adjective "takai (*expensive*)" is conjugated.

	Informal	Formal
Present	**takai**	**takai desu**
Present Negative	**takaku nai**	**takaku nai desu** **takaku arimasen**
Past	**'takakatta**	**takakatta desu**
Past Negative	**takaku nakatta**	**takaku nakatta desu** **takaku arimasen deshita**

There is only one exception to the rule of i-adjectives, which is "ii (*good*)". "Ii" derives from "yoi," and its conjugation is mostly based on "yoi".

	Informal	Formal
Present	**ii**	**ii desu**
Present Negative	**yoku nai**	**yoku nai desu**
		yoku arimasen
Past	**yokatta**	**yokatta desu**
Past negative	**yoku nakatta**	**yoku nakatta desu**
		yoku arimasen deshita

Na-Adjectives as Predicates

They are called na-adjectives because "~ na" marks this group of adjectives when directly modifying noun (*e.g. yuumeina gaka*). Unlike i-adjectives, na-adjectives cannot be used as predicates themselves. When a na-adjective is used as a predicate, the final "na" is deleted and followed by either "~ da" or "~ desu (*in formal speech*)". As with nouns, "~ da" or "~ desu" changes its form to express the past tense, the negative, and the affirmative.

	Informal	Formal
Present	**yuumei da**	**yuumei desu**
Present Negative	**yuumei dewa nai**	**yuumei dewa**

		arimasen
Past	**yuumei datta**	**yuumei deshita**
Past negative	**yuumei dewa nakatta**	**yuumei dewa arimasen deshita**

Lessson 11

Personal Pronouns

A pronoun is a word that takes the place of a noun. The use of Japanese personal pronouns is quite different from English. They are not used as often as their English counterparts, though there are a variety of pronouns in Japanese depending on the gender or the style of speech.

If the context is clear, the Japanese prefer not to use the personal pronouns. It is important to learn how to use them, but also important to understand how not to use them. Unlike English, there is no strict rule to have a grammatical subject in a sentence.

Here are some of the Japanese pronouns.

I	you	
watakushi	**otaku**	very formal
watashi	**anata**	formal
boku (male), **atashi** (female)	**kimi** (male)	informal

ore (male)	**omae** (male), **anta**	very informal

Among these pronouns, "watashi" and "anata" are the most common. However, they are often omitted in conversation. When addressing your superior, "anata" is not appropriate and should be avoided. Use the person's name instead.

"Anata" is also used by wives when they address their husbands. "Omae" is sometimes used by husbands when addressing their wives, though it sounds a little bit old-fashioned.

The pronouns for the third person are "kare (*he*)" or "kanojo (*she*)." Rather than using these words, it is preferred to use the person's name or describe them as "ano hito (*that person*)." It is not necessary to include gender.

Kyo John ni aimashita.	I saw him (John) today.
Ano hito o shitte imasu ka.	Do you know her?

"Kare" or "kanojo" often means a boyfriend or a girlfriend.

Kare ga imasu ka.	Do you have a boyfriend?
Watashi no kanojo wa kangofu desu.	My girlfriend is a nurse.

To make plurals, a suffix "~ tachi" is added like "watashi-tachi (we)" or "anata-tachi (you)". The suffix "~ tachi" can be added to not only pronouns but to some other nouns referring to people. For example, "kodomo-tachi" means "children."

For the word "anata," the suffix "~ gata" is used sometimes to make it plural instead of using "~ tachi." "Anata-gata" is more formal than "anata-tachi." The suffix "~ ra" is also used for "kare," such as "karera (they)."

Lesson 12

Particles

Particles are probably one of the most difficult and confusing aspects of Japanese sentences. A particle (joshi) is a word that shows the relationship of a word, a phrase, or a clause to the rest of the sentence. Some particles have English equivalents. Others have functions similar to English prepositions, but since they always follow the word or words they mark, they are post-positions. There are also particles that have a peculiar usage which is not found in English. Most particles are multi-functional.

Particles: Wa and Ga

Particles are probably one of the most difficult and confusing aspects of Japanese sentences. Among particles, the question often asked is about the use of "wa" and "ga." They seems to make many people confused, but don't be intimidated by them! Let's have a look at the functions of these particles.

Topic Marker and Subject Marker

Roughly speaking, "wa" is a topic marker, and "ga" is a subject marker. The topic is often the same as the subject, but not necessary. The topic can be anything that a speaker wants to talk about (*It can be an object, location or any other grammatical element*). In this sense, it is similar to the English expressions, "As for ~" or "Speaking of ~."

Watashi wa gakusei desu.	I am a student. (*As for me, I am a student.*)
Nihongo wa omoshiroi desu.	Japanese is interesting. (*Speaking of Japanese, it is interesting.*)

Basic Differences Between Ga and Wa

"Wa" is used to mark something that has already been introduced into the conversation, or is familiar with both a speaker and a listener. (*proper nouns, genetic names etc.*) "Ga" is used when a situation or happening is just noticed or newly introduced. See the following example.

Mukashi mukashi, ojii-san ga sunde imashita. Ojii-san wa totemo shinsetsu deshita.	Once upon a time, there lived an old man. He was very kind.

In the first sentence, "ojii-san" is introduced for the first time. It is the subject, not the topic. The second sentence describes about "ojii-san" that is previously mentioned.

"Ojii-san" is now the topic, and is marked with "wa" instead of "ga."

Wa as Contrast

Beside being a topic marker, "wa" is used to show contrast or to emphasize the subject.

Biiru wa nomimasu ga, wain wa nomimasen.	I drink beer, but I don't drink wine.

The thing being contrasted may or may not stated, but with this usage, the contrast is implied.

Ano hon wa yomimasen deshita.	I didn't read that book (*though I read this one*).

Particles such as "ni," "de," "kara" and "made" can be combined with "wa" (*double particles*) to show contrast.

Osaka ni wa ikimashita ga, Kyoto ni wa ikimasen deshita.	I went to Osaka, but I didn't go to Kyoto.
Koko de wa tabako o suwanaide kudasai.	Please don't smoke here (*but you may smoke there*).

Whether "wa" indicates a topic or a contrast, it depends on the context or the intonation.

Ga with Question Words

When a question word such as "who" and "what" is the subject of a sentence, it is always followed by "ga," never by "wa." To answer the question, it also has to be followed by "ga."

Dare ga kimasu ka.   Who is coming?

Yoko ga kimasu.   Yoko is coming.

Ga as Emphasis

"Ga" is used for emphasis, to distinguish a person or thing from all others. If a topic is marked with "wa," the comment is the most important part of the sentence. On the other hand, if a subject is marked with "ga," the subject is the most important part of the sentence. In English, these differences are sometimes expressed in tone of voice. Compare these sentences.

Taro wa gakkou ni ikimashita.   Taro went to school.

Taro ga gakkou ni ikimashita.   Taro is the one who went to school.

Ga in a Special Circumstance

The object of the sentence is usually marked by the particle "o," but some verbs and adjectives (*expressing like/dislike, desire, potential, necessity, fear, envy etc.*) take "ga" instead of "o."

Kuruma ga hoshii desu.   I want a car.

Nihongo ga wakarimasu.   I understand Japanese.

Ga in Subordinate Clauses

The subject of a subordinate clause normally takes "ga" to show that the subjects of the subordinate and main clauses are different.

Watashi wa Mika ga kekkon shita koto o shiranakatta.

I didn't know that Mika got married.

LESSON 13

Particles: O and No

    Particles are probably one of the most difficult and confusing aspects of Japanese sentences. A particle (*joshi*) is a word that shows the relationship of a word, a phrase, or a clause to the rest of the sentence. Some particles have English equivalents. Others have functions similar to English prepositions, but since they always follow the word or words they mark, they are post-positions. There are also particles that have a peculiar usage which is not found in English. Most particles are multi-functional.

The Particle "O"

Direct Object Marker

"O" is placed after a noun, and indicates that the noun is the direct object.

Kinou eiga o mimashita.	I watched the movie yesterday.
Kutsu o kaimashita.	I bought shoes.

Route of Motion

Verbs such as walk, run, pass, turn, drive, go through etc., take the particle "o" to indicate the route which the movement follows.

Basu wa toshokan no mae o toorimasu.	The bus passes in front of the library.
Tsugi no kado o magatte kudasai.	Please turn the next corner.

Point of Departure

Verbs such as leave, come out, get off etc., take the particle "o" to mark the place from which one gets of or leaves.

Hachi-ji ni ie o demasu.	I leave home at eight o'clock.
Kyonen koukou o sotsugyou shimashita.	I graduated from high school last year.

The Particle "No"

Possessive Marker

"No" indicates ownership or attribution. It is similar to the English "apostrophe s ('s)."

Kore wa watashi no hon desu.	This is my book.
Watashi no ane wa Tokyo ni sunde imasu.	My sister lives in Tokyo.

The final noun can be omitted if it is clear to both speaker and listener.

Are wa watashi no (*kuruma*) desu.	That is mine (*my car*).

Noun Modification

The noun before "no" modifies the noun after "no". This usage is similar to the possessive, but it is seen more with compound nouns or noun phrases. (*e.g. kono hon no chosha -> the author of this book*)

Nihongo no jugyou wa tanoshii desu.	The Japanese class is interesting.
Bijutsu no hon o sagashite imasu.	I am looking for a book on fine arts.

"No" can be used many times in one sentence. In this usage the order of nouns in Japanese is the reverse of the English structure. The normal Japanese order is from large to small, or general to specific.

Osaka daigaku no nihongo no sensei	a teacher of Japanese at Osaka university
yooroppa no kuni no namae	the names of the countries in Europe

Apposition

"No" links the noun to the appositive that follows.

Tomodachi no Keiko-san desu.	This is my friend, Keiko.

Bengoshi no Tanaka-san wa itsumo isogashisou da.

The lawyer, Mr. Tanaka seems to be busy all the time.

Lesson 14

The Particle :Ni

Indirect Object Marker

An indirect object usually precedes a direct object.

Yoku tomodachi ni tegami o kakimasu.	I often write letters to my friends.
Kare wa watashi ni hon	He gave me a book.

Some Japanese verbs such as "au (*to meet*)" and "kiku (*to ask*)" take an indirect object, though their English counterparts do not.

Eki de tomodachi ni atta.	I met my friend at the station.

Location of Existence

"Ni" is typically used with verbs such as "iru (*to exist*)," "aru (*to exist*)" and "sumu (*to live*)." It translates into "at" or "in."

Isu no ue ni neko ga imasu.	There is a cat on the chair.
Ryoushin wa Osaka ni sunde imasu.	My parents live in Osaka.

Direct Contract

"Ni" is used when a motion or action is directed at or onto an object or place.

Koko ni namae o kaite kudasai.	Please write your name here.
Kooto o hangaa ni kaketa.	I hung a coat on the hanger.

Direction

"Ni" can be translated as "to" when indicating a destination.

Rainen nihon ni ikimasu.	I'm going to Japan next year.
Kinou ginkou ni ikimashita.	I went to the bank yesterday.

Purpose

Eiga o mi ni itta.	I went to see a movie.
Hirugohan o tabe ni uchi ni kaetta.	I went home to eat lunch.

Specific Time

"Ni" is used with various time expressions (*year, month, day, and clock time*) to indicate a specific point in time, and translates into "at," "on," or "in." However, the expressions of relative time such as today, tomorrow don't take the particle "ni."

Hachiji ni ie o demasu.	I leave home at eight o'clock.
Gogatsu mikka ni umaremashita.	I was born on May 3rd.

Source

"Ni" indicates an agent or a source in passive or causative verbs. It translates into "by" or "from".

Haha ni shikarareta.	I was scolded by my mother.
Tomu ni eigo o oshietemoratta.	I was taught English by Tom.

Notion of Per

"Ni" is used with frequency expressions such as per hour, per day, per person, etc.

**Ichijikan ni juu-doru
haratte kuremasu.**

They pay us
ten dollars per
hour.

**Isshukan ni sanjuu-jikan
hatarakimasu.**

I work 30 hours
per week.

Lesson 15

The Particle : De

Place of Action

It indicates the place where an action takes place. It translates into "in", "at", "on", and so on.

Depaato de kutsu o katta.
I bought shoes at the department store.

Umi de oyoida.
I swam in the ocean.

Means

It indicates means, method, or instruments. It translates into "by", "with", "in" "by means of", etc.

Basu de gakkou ni ikimasu.	I go to school by bus.
Nihongo de hanashite kudasai.	Please speak in Japanese.

Totalizing

It is placed after a quantity, time or amount of money, and indicates an extent.

San-nin de kore o tsukutta.	Three of us made this.
Zenbu de sen-en desu.	They cost 1,000 yen altogether.

Scope

It translates into "in", "among", "within", etc.

Kore wa sekai de	This is the biggest in the world.
Nihon de doko ni ikitai desu ka. ichiban ookii desu.	Where do you want to go in Japan?

Time Limit

It indicates time consumed for a certain action or occurrence. It translates into "in", "within", etc.

Ichijikan de ikemasu.	We can get there in an hour.

Isshuukan de dekimasu.

I can do it in a week.

Material

It indicates the composition of an object.

Toufu wa daizu de tsukurimasu.

Tofu is made from soybeans.

Kore wa nendo de tsukutta hachi desu.

This is a bowl made of clay.

Required Cost

It translates into "for", "at", etc.

Kono hon o juu-doru de katta.

I bought this book for ten dollars.

Kore wa ikura de okuremasu ka.

How much would it cost to send this?

Cause

It indicates a casual reason or motive for an action or occurrence. It translates into "due to", "because of", "owing to", etc.

Kaze de gakkou o yasunda.

I was absent from school due to a cold.

Fuchuui de kaidan kara ochita.   I fell down the
stairs
due to
carelessness.

Lesson 16

The Particle : To

Complete Listing

It connects only nouns and pronouns, never phrases and clauses. It translates into "and".

Kutsu to boushi o katta.	I bought shoes and a hat.
Eigo to nihongo o hanashimasu.	I speak English and Japanese.

Contrast

It indicates a comparison or contrast between the two nouns.

Neko to inu to dochira ga suki desu ka.	Which do you like better, cats or dogs?

Accompaniment

It translates into "together, with".

Tomodachi to eiga ni itta.	I went to a movie with my friend.
Yuki wa raigetsu Ichiro to kekkon shimasu.	Yuki is going to marry Ichiro next month.

Change/Result

It is commonly used in the phrase "~ to naru", and indicates that something reaches a goal or new state.

Tsuini orinpikku no kaisai no hi to natta.	At last the opening day of the Olympics has come.
Bokin wa zenbu de hyakuman-en to natta.	The total amount of donations reached one million yen.

Quotation

It is used before such verbs as "~ iu", "~ omou", "~ kiku", *etc.* to introduce a clause or a phrase. It is normally preceded by a plain form of a verb.

Kare wa asu kuru to itta.	He said that he will come tomorrow.

Rainen nihon ni ikou to

I am thinking of going to Japan next year.

Conditional

It is placed after a verb or an adjective to form a conditional. It translates into "as soon as," "when," "if," *etc.* A plain form is usually used before the particle "to".

Shigoto ga owaru to sugu uchi ni kaetta.

I went home as soon as work was over.

Ano mise ni iku to oishii sushi ga taberareru.

If you go to that restaurant, you can have great sushi.

Sound Symbolism

It is used after onomatopoeic adverbs.

Hoshi ga kira kira to kag

Th rs are

Kodomotachi wa bata bata to hashirimawatta.

n ran around making lots of noise.

Lesson 17

Sentence Ending Particle

In Japanese, there are many particles that are added to the end of a sentence. They express the speaker's emotions, doubt, emphasis, caution, hesitation, wonder, admiration, and so on. Some sentence ending particles distinguish male or female speech. Many of them don't translate easily.

Ka

Makes a sentence into a question. When forming a question, the word order of a sentence does not change in Japanese.

Nihon-jin desu ka.	Are you Japanese?
Supeingo o hanashimasu ka.	Do you speak Spanish?

Kana/Kashira

Indicates that you are not sure about something. It can be translated as "I wonder ~". "Kashira" is used only by women.

Tanaka-san wa ashita kuru kana.	I wonder if Mr. Tanaka will come tomorrow.
Ano hito wa dare kashira.	I wonder who that person is.

Na

(1) Prohibition. A negative imperative marker used only by men in very informal speech.

Sonna koto o suru na!	Don't do such a thing!

(2) Casual emphasis on a decision, suggestion or opinion.

Kyou wa shigoto ni ikitakunai na.	I don't want to go to work today.
Sore wa machigatteiru to omou na.	I think that is wrong.

Naa

Expresses emotion, or a casual remark of wishful thinking.

Sugoi naa.	How great it is!
Mou sukoshi nete itai naa.	I wish I could sleep in a little more.

Ne/Nee

Conformation. Indicates that the speaker wants the listener to agree or confirm. It is similar to English expressions "don't you think so", "isn't it?" or "right?"

Ii tenki desu ne.	It's a beautiful day, isn't it?
Mou nakanaide ne.	Please don't cry anymore, okay?

No

(1) Indicates an explanation or emotive emphasis. Used only by women or children in an informal situation.

Kore jibunde tsukutta no.	I made this myself.
Onaka ga itai no.	I have stomachache.

(2) Makes a sentence into a question (*with a rising intonation*). Informal version of "~ no desu ka".

Ashita konai no?	Aren't you coming tomorrow?
Doushita no?	What's the matter with you?

Sa

Emphasizes the sentence. Used mainly by men.

Sonna koto wa wakatteiru sa.	I certainly know of such a thing.
Hajime kara umaku dekinai no wa atarimae sa.	It's natural (*indeed*) that

you can't do well when you first starts.

Wa

Used only by women. It can have both an emphatic function and a softening effect.

Watashi ga suru wa.	I'll do it.
Sensei ni kiita hou ga ii to omou wa.	I think it would be better to ask the teacher.

Yo

(1) Emphasizes a command.

Benkyou shinasai yo!	Study!
Okoranaide yo!	Don't get so angry at me!

(2) Indicates moderate emphasis, especially useful when the speaker provides a new piece of information.

Ano eiga wa sugoku yokatta yo.	That movie was very good.
Kare wa tabako o suwanai yo.	He doesn't smoke, you know.

Ze

Elicits an agreement. Used only by men in casual conversation among colleagues, or with those whose social status is below that of the speaker.

Nomi ni ikou ze.   Let's go for a
                         drink!

Zo

Emphasizes one's opinion or judgment. Used mainly by
men.

Iku zo.   I'm going!

Kore wa omoi zo.   This is heavy, I tell
                         you.

Lesson 18

Specificity of Japanese Verbs

Some Japanese verbs are more specific when describing actions than English verbs. While there is only one verb used for a certain action in English, there might be several different verbs in Japanese. One of the examples is the verb "to wear." In English, it can used as, "I wear a hat," "I wear gloves," "I wear glasses" and so on. However, Japanese has different verbs depending on which part of the body it will be worn on. Let's take a look how the Japanese describe "to wear."

Boushi o kaburu.   I wear a hat.
(*"Kaburu" is used to put on the head.*)

Megane o kakeru.   I wear glasses.

(*"Kakeru" also means, "to hang."*)

Iyaringu o tsukeru.   I wear earrings.
(*"Tsukeru" also means, "to attach."*)

Nekutai o shimeru. I wear a tie.
(*"Shimeru" also means, "to tie."*)

Sukaafu o maku. I wear scarf.
(*Maku" also means, "to wrap around."*)

Tebukuro o hameru. I wear gloves.
(*"Hameru" also means, "to insert."*)

Yubiwa o hameru. I wear rings.

Tokei o suru. I wear a watch.

Shatsu o kiru. I wear shirts.
(*"Kiru" is used to put on the body.*)

Zubon o haku. I wear pants.
(*"Haku" is used to put on the legs.*)

Kutsu o haku. I wear shoes.
(*"Haku" is also used to put on footwear.*)

Another example is the verb "to play."

Omocha de asobu. I play with toys.
(*"Asobu" originally means,
"to amuse oneself."*)

Piano o hiku. I play the piano.
(*"Hiku" is used to play the
musical instrument that requires
the manipulation of fingers.*)

Fue o fuku. I play the flute.
(*"Fuku" is used to play the musical
instrument that requires blowing.*)

Taiko o tataku. I play the drum.
(*"Tataku" is used to play the
musical instrument that requires beating.*)

Rekoodo o kakeru.

Rekoodo o kakeru.

I am playing a record.

Toranpu o suru.

I play cards.

Yakyuu o suru.
(*"Suru" can be used for most sports.*)

I play baseball.

Romio o enjiru.

I play the role of Romeo.

Lesson 19

Extended use of the verb "Suru"

The verb "suru (*to do*)" has many extended uses that occur quite often.

To make

(a) Adverb form of I-adjective + suru
To change I-adjective to adverb form, replace the final ~i with ~ku. (*e.g. ookii > ookiku*)

Terebi no oto o ookiku shita.   I turned up the volume of the TV.

(b) Adverb form of Na-adjective + suru
To change Na-adjective to adverb form, replace the final ~na with ~ni. (*e.g. kireina > kireini*)

Heya o kireini suru.
I'm cleaning the room.

To decide

It should be used when you are choosing from several available alternatives.

Koohii ni shimasu.
I'll have coffee.

Kono tokei ni shimasu.
I'll take this watch.

To price

When accompanied by phrases indicating prices, it means "cost."

Kono kaban wa gosen en shimashita.
This bag cost 5,000 yen.

To feel, to smell, or to hear

Ii nioi ga suru.
It smells good.

Nami no oto ga suru.
I hear the sound of the waves.

Loan word + suru

The loan words are often combined with "suru" to change the word into a verb.

doraibu suru to drive   **taipu suru** to type

kisu suru to kiss   **nokku suru** to knock

Noun (of Chinese origin) + *suru*

It is combined with nouns of Chinese origin to make a noun into a verb.

benkyou suru	to study	**sentaku suru**	to do the washing
ryokou suru	to travel	**shitsumon suru**	to ask questions
denwa suru	to telephone	**yakusoku suru**	to promise
sanpo suru	to take a walk	**yoyaku suru**	to reserve
shokuji suru	to have a meal	**souji suru**	to clean
kekkon suru	to get married	**kaimono suru**	to shop
setsumei suru	to explain	**junbi suru**	to prepare

The particle "o" can be used as an object particle after a noun. (*e.g.* "*benkyou o suru*," "*denwa o suru*") There is no difference in meaning with or without "o."

Adverb or Onomatopoeic expression + *suru*

Adverb or onomatopoeic expression can be combined with "suru" to change them into verbs.

yukkuri	to stay long	**bonyari**	to be
suru		**suru**	absent
			minded
niko niko	to smile	**waku**	to be
suru		**waku**	excited
		suru	

Lesson 20

Conversation Openers and Fillers

In conversations, openers and fillers are used quite often. They don't always have specific meanings. Openers are used as signals that you are about to say something, or to smooth communication. Fillers are usually used for pauses or hesitation. English also has similar expressions such as "so," "like," "you know," and so on. When you have opportunity to hear native speakers' conversation, listen carefully and examine how and when they are used. Here are some openers and fillers frequently used.

Marking a new topic

Sore de	So
De	So (*informal*)

Saying something off the topic

Tokorode	By the way

Hanashi wa chigaimasu ga	To change the subject
Hanashi chigau kedo	To change the subject (*informal*)

Adding to the current topic

Tatoeba	For example
Iikaereba	In other words
Souieba	Speaking of
Gutaiteki ni iu to	More concretely

Bringing up the main topic

Jitsu wa	The fact is, To tell the truth

Shortening the preliminary topics

Sassoku desu ga	May I come straight to the point?

Introducing someone or something you have just noticed

A, Aa, Ara	"ara" is mainly used by female speakers.

Note: "Aa" can also be used to show that you understand.

Hesitation Sounds

Ano, Anou	Used to get the listener's attention.
Eeto	Let me see ...

Ee   Uhh ...

Maa   Well, say ...

Asking for repetition

E
(*with a rising intonation*)   What?

Haa   What? (*informal*)
(*with a rising intonation*)

Lesson 21

Counters

Each language has different ways of counting objects. Japanese uses counters. They are similar to English expressions such as "a cup of ~," "a sheet of ~" and so on. There are a variety of counters, often based on the shape of the object. The counters are attached directly to a number (*e.g. ni-hai, san-mai*). If you are not familiar with Japanese numbers. When combining a number with a counter, the pronunciation of the number or the counter might change. When grouping objects, Japanese divide them into groups of five and ten unlike six and twelve in the West. For example, sets of Japanese dishes or bowls are sold in units of five. Traditionally, there was no word for dozen, though it has been used because of Western influence.

Objects

hon	Long, cylindrical objects: trees, pens, etc.
mai	Flat, thin objects: paper, stamps, dishes, etc.

ko	Broad category of small and compact objects
hai	Liquid in cups, glasses, bowls, etc.
satsu	Bound objects: books, magazines, etc.
dai	Vehicles, machines etc.
kai	The floor of a building
ken	Houses, buildings
soku	Pairs of footwear: sock, shoes, etc.
tsuu	Letters

Things which are not clearly categorized or shapeless are counted by using native Japanese numbers.

Duration

jikan	Hour, as in "ni-jikan (*two hours*)"
fun	Minute, as in "go-fun (*five minutes*)"
byoo	Second, as in "sanjuu-byoo (*thirty seconds*)"
shuukan	Week, as in "san-shuukan (*three weeks*)"
kagetsu	Month, as in "ni-kagetsu (*two months*)"
nenkan	Year, as in "juu-nenkan (*ten years*)"

Animals

hiki	Insects, fish, small animals: cats, dogs, etc.
tou	Large animals: horses, bears, etc.
wa	Birds

Frequency

kai	Times, as in "ni-kai (*twice*)"
do	Times, as in "ichi-do (*once*)"

Order

ban Ordinal numbers, as in "ichi-ban (*first place, number one*)"

tou Class, grade, as in "san-too (*third place*)"

People

nin "Hitori (*one person*)" and "futari (*two people*)" are exceptions.

mei More formal than "nin."

Others

sai Age, as in "go-sai (*five years old*)"

When using a counter, pay attention to the word order. It is different from English order. A typical order is "noun + particle + quantity = verbs." Here are examples.

Hon o ni-satsu kaimashita I bought two books.

Koohii o ni-hai kudasai. Please give me two cups of coffee.

Lesson 22

Expression of Desire

There are two ways to express desire or wish. When what one desires takes a noun (*I want a car, I want money etc.*) "hoshii (*to want*)" is used. When what one's wants involve action (*I want to go, I want to eat etc.*), the stem of the verb + "~ tai" is used.

Kuruma ga hoshii desu.	I want a car.
Kuruma o kaitai desu.	I want to buy a car.
Sono hon ga hoshii desu.	I want that book.
Sono hon o yomitai desu.	I want to read that book.

In informal situations, "~ desu" can be omitted.

Okane ga hoshii.	I want money.
Nihon ni ikitai.	I want to go to Japan.

These patters are used only for the first person, and in question for the second person. When describing a third person's desire, "hoshigatte imasu" or the stem of the verb + "~ tagatte imasu" are used.

Kamera ga hoshii desu.	I want a camera.
Ani wa kamera o hoshigatte imasu.	My brother wants a camera.
Kono eiga o mitai desu.	I want to watch this movie.
Ken wa kono eiga o mitagatte imasu.	Ken wants to watch this movie.

Please note that the object of "hoshii" is marked with the particle "ga," while the object of "hoshigatte imasu" is marked with the particle "o." The "~ tai" expression is not normally used when asking about the desire of one's superior.

Lesson 23

Expression of Ability

    Ability and potential can be expressed by two different ways.

(1) Attaching the phrase "~ koto ga dekiru" after the basic form of the verb. Literally "koto" means "thing," and "dekiru" means "can do." The formal form of "~ koto ga dekiru" is "~ koto ga dekimasu," and past tense is "~ koto ga dekita (~ *koto ga dekimashita*)."

Nihongo o hanasu koto ga dekiru.	I can speak Japanese.
Piano o hiku koto ga dekimasu.	I can play piano.
Yuube yoku neru koto ga dekita.	I could sleep well last night.

"~ dekiru" can be directly attached to a noun, if a verb is closely associated with its direct object.

Nihongo ga dekiru.	I can speak Japanese.
Piano ga dekimasu.	I can play piano.

(2) By potential form of the verb. Potential verb forms are formed as shown below.

	Basic form	Potential form
U-verbs:	**iku** (to go)	**ikeru**
replace the final "~u" with "~eru".	**kaku** (to write)	**kakeru**
RU-verbs:	**miru** (to see)	**mirareru**
replace the final "~ru" with "~rareru".	**taberu** (to eat)	**taberareru**
Irregular verbs	**kuru** (to come)	**koreru**
	suru (to do)	**dekiru**

In informal conversation, "~ra" is often dropped from potential form of RU-verbs. For example, "mireru" and "tabereru" instead of "mirareru" and "taberareru."

The potential form of the verb can be replaced with the form using "~ koto ga dekiru." It is more colloquial and less formal to use the potential form of the verb.

Supeingo o hanasu koto ga dekiru.	I can speak Spanish.
Supeingo o hanaseru.	
Sashimi o taberu koto ga dekiru.	I can eat raw fish.
Sashimi o taberareu.	

Lesson 24

Expressing Uncertainty

There are several ways to express uncertainty. "~ darou" is a plain form of "~ deshou," and means "will probably." The adverb "tabun (*perhaps*)" is sometimes added.

Kare wa ashita kuru deshou.	He will probably come tomorrow.
Ashita wa hareru darou.	It will be sunny tomorrow.
Kyo haha wa tabun uchi ni iru deshou.	My mother will probably be home today.

"~ darou" or "~deshou" is also used to form a tag question. In this case you usually can tell the meaning from the context.

Tsukareta deshou.	You were tired, weren't you?
Kyo wa kyuuryoubi darou.	Today is a payday, isn't it?

"~ darou ka" or "~ deshou ka" is used when guessing with doubt. "~ kashira" is used only by females. A similar expression used by both genders is "~ kana," though it is informal. These expressions are close to "I wonder ~" in English.

Emi wa mou igirisu ni itta no darou ka.	I wonder if Emi has already gone to England.
Kore ikura kashira.	I wonder how much this is.
Nobu wa itsu kuru no kana.	I wonder when Nobu will come.

"~ kamoshirenai" is used to express a sense of probability or doubt. It shows even more uncertainty than "~ darou" or "~ deshou". It is used when you don't know all the facts and are often just guessing. It is similar to the English expression "might be." The formal version of "~ kamoshirenai" is "kamoshiremasen".

Ashita wa ame kamoshirenai.	It might rain tomorrow.
Kinyoubi desu kara, kondeiru kamoshiremasen.	Since it is Friday, it might be busy.
Kare wa tabun kin-medaru o toru deshou.	He will probably get the gold medal.
Kare wa kin-medal o totta no kana.	I wonder if he got the gold medal.
Kare wa kin-medaru o toru kamoshirenai.	He might get the gold medal.

The last thing to mention is, "~ darou" or "~ deshou" can't be used when referring to one's own actions, though "~ kamoshirenai" can be used in these situations.

Ashita watashi wa Kobe ni iku kamoshirenai.	I might go to Kobe tomorrow.
Ashita watashi wa Kobe ni iku darou.	**Wrong**
Ashita ane wa Kobe ni iku darou.	My sister will go to Kobe tomorrow.

Lesson 25

Expressing Apologies

The Japanese typically apologize far more frequently than Westerners. This probably results from cultural differences between them. Westerners seem reluctant to admit their own failure. Since apologizing means that admitting one's own failure or guilt, it may not be best thing to do if the problem is to be resolved in a court of law.

Apologizing is considered a virtue in Japan. Apologies show that a person takes responsibility and avoids blaming others. When one apologizes and shows one's remorse, the Japanese are more willing to forgive. There are much less court cases in Japan compared to the States. When apologizing the Japanese often bow. The more you feel sorry, the more deeply you bow. Here are some expressions used to apologize.

Sumimasen.

It is probably the most common phrase used to apologize. Some people say it as "Suimasen". Since "Sumimasen" can be used in several different situations (when requesting something, when thanking someone etc.), listen carefully to what the context is. If you are apologizing that something has been done, "Sumimasen deshita" can be used.

Moushiwake arimasen.

Very formal expression. It should be used to superiors. It shows a stronger feeling than "Sumimasen". If you are apologizing that something has been done, "Moushiwake arimasen deshita" can be used. Like "Sumimasen", "Moushiwake arimasen" is also used to express gratitude.

Shitsurei shimashita.

Formal expression, but it doesn't show as strong a feeling as "Moushiwake arimasen".

Gomennasai.

Common phrase. Unlike "Sumimasen," the usage is limited to apologizing. Since it is less formal and has a childish ring to it, it is not appropriate to use to superiors.

Shitsurei.

Casual. It is mostly used by men. It also can be used as "Excuse me".

Doomo.

Casual. It also can be used as "Thanks".

Gomen.

Very casual. Adding a sentence ending particle, "Gomen ne" or "Gomen na (male speech) is also used. It should be only used with close friends or family members.

Lesson 26

Quantity Expressions

Quantity expressions are used as adverbial phrases. The word order is generally **noun + particle + quantity + verb**. When they are used to modify adjectives, they come just before the adjective. For example, "very hot" is "totemo atsui".

Here are some quantity expressions that are frequently used.

takusan	many, much
totemo	very
kanari	considerably, rather
sukoshi	a little, a few
chotto	a little (*Less formal than "sukoshi"*)

Learn how they are used in the sentences.

Hon o takusan yomimau.

I read many books.

Totemo oishii desu.

It is very delicious.

Jikan ga kanari kakaru deshou.

It will take quite a long time.

Nihongo o sukoshi hanashimasu.

I speak a little Japanese.

Piano o chotto hiku koto ga dekimasu.

I can play piano a little bit.

Here are some quantity expressions used only in negative sentences.

amari	(*not*) very, (*not*) much
zenzen	(*not*) at all

Here are some sample sentences.

Amari chigai ga arimasen.	There is not much difference.
Zenzen yokunakatta desu.	It was not good at all.

Lesson 27

Expressing one's thought

When expressing one's thought, feelings, opinions, ideas and guesses, "~ to omou (I think that ~)" is frequently used. The particle "to" indicates that the preceding sentence or words are a quotation.

Since "~ to omou" always refers to the speaker's thoughts, "watashi wa" is normally omitted.

Ashita ame ga furu to omoimasu.	I think it will rain tomorrow.
Kono kuruma wa takai to omou.	I think this car is expensive.
Kare wa furansu-jin da to omou.	I think he is French.
Kono kangae o dou omoimasu ka.	What do you think about this idea?

Totemo ii to omoimasu. I think it is very good.

If the content of the quoted clause expresses one's intention or speculation about a future event or state, a volitional form of a verb is used preceding "~ to omou." To express a thought other than one's volition or opinion toward the future, a plain form of a verb or adjective is used preceding "~ to omou" as shown in the examples above.

Oyogi ni ikou to omou. I think I'm going to swim.

Ryokou ni tsuite kakou to omou. I think I will write about my trip.

To express a thought or idea you have at the time of your statement, "~ to omotte iru (I am thinking that ~)" is used rather than "~ to omou."

Haha ni denwa o shiyou to I'm thinking of.

omotte imasu. calling my mom.

Rainen nihon ni ikou to omotte imasu. I'm thinking of going to Japan next year.

Atarashii kuruma o kaitai to omotte imasu. I'm thinking that I want to buy a new car.

When the subject is a third person, "~ to omotte iru" is used exclusively.

Kare wa kono shiai ni kateru to omotte iru. He thinks he can win this game.

Unlike English, the negation "I don't think" is normally placed within the quoted clause. It is possible to negate "~ to omou" such as "~ to omowanai," however, it expresses stronger doubt, and is close to the English "I doubt that ~."

Maki wa ashita konai to omoimasu.	I don't think Maki is coming tomorrow.
Nihongo wa muzukashikunai to omou.	I don't think Japanese is difficult.

Lesson 28

Expressing Pleasure and Sadness

Expressing your emotions is an important part of communication. Adjectives are used when expressing emotions.

Ureshii	glad, happy
Shiawasena	happy, fortunate
Zannenna	unfortunate, disappointing
Kanashii	sad
Sabishii	lonely

Emotions are usually expressed straightforwardly; therefore informal speeches are widely used. Here are some useful expressions.

Ureshii naa. (M)	I am glad!
Ureshii wa. (F)	
Shiawase da naa. (M)	I am happy!
Shiawase da wa. (F)	

Zannen da naa. (M)　　　　I am sorry to hear
Zannen nee. (F)　　　　　that.

Kanashii naa. (M)　　　　I am sad.
Kanashii wa. (F)

Sabishii naa. (M)　　　　I am lonely.
Sabishii wa. (F)

When describing someone's emotions, "~sou desu (*looks, seems*)" is added to the stem of the adjective.

Yuki wa shiawase sou desu.　　Yuki looks happy.

**Chichi wa totemo sabishi
sou deshita.**　　　　　My father seemed
　　　　　　　　very lonely.

Lesson 29

Expressing Interjections and Exclamations

    You will need quite a bit of experience in, and understanding of, a culture to speak its language naturally. If the proper expression does not come to mind instantly, it will sound like you are reading it. When you have a chance to hear the Japanese speaking, listen carefully to the way they speak as well as to their facial expressions. If you are interested in these exclamatory expressions, the Japanese comic books (*manga*), which include many of them, might be good a resource to explore.

Here are the expressions widely used. Remember that exclamations are used almost always in informal style.

A, Aa Oh.	**A, nagareboshi da!** Oh, that's a shooting star!
Aree, Oya, Maa Oh my! Gee!	**Maa kirei na nagame nee!** Oh my, what a nice view!

("Maa" is used by women only.)

E	**E, Shigoto yameta no.**
What?	What, you quit your job?
Masaka!	**Masaka sonna koto ga aruhazu nai yo!**
No kidding!	That can't be happened!
Hee!	**Hee, sore wa yokatta ne!**
Really!	Wow, that's great!
Naruhodo	**Naruhodo, sou iu koto datta no ka.**
I see.	I see, that's the way it was.
Yare yare	**Yare yare, nante koto da!**
Oh boy!	Oh boy, what a disaster!

Lesson 30

Greetings for special occasions

Greeting with appropriate words is important for socializing. Here are some useful expressions for special occasions.

Celebration

Omedetou gozaimasu.   Congratulations.

Omedetou. (*casual*)

The form "gozaimasu" is more polite. It is added when you are talking with somebody who is not a family members or a close friend. To reply, "Arigatou gozaimasu" or "Arigatou" is used.

O-tanjoubi omedetou   Happy Birthday.
gozaimasu. (*formal*)

Tanjoubi omedetou. (*casual*)

Go-kekkon omedetou gozaimasu. (*formal*)

Congratulations on your wedding.

Kekkon omedetou. (*casual*)

The honorific "o" or "go" can be attached to the front of some nouns as a formal way of saying "your". It is very polite.

To somebody who is sick

Guai wa ikaga desu ka.

How are you feeling?
(*Literally means, How is your condition?*)

Kaze wa dou desu ka.

How is your cold?

Okagesama de yoku narimashita.

Thanks to your help, I have gotten better.

"Okagesama de" can be used whenever you announce good news in answer to someone's concerned inquiry.

Odaiji ni.

Please take care of yourself.

To reply "Odaiji ni", "Arigatou gozaimasu" is used.

Seeing someone after a long absence

Gobusata shite imasu.
(*very formal*)

I haven't seen you in a long time.

Ohisashiburi desu. (*formal*)   Long time no see.

Hisashiburi!
(*casual*)

There is a Japanese song titled "Ohisashiburi ne". "Ne" is a sentence particle. Ne is used to seek confirmation and is similar to English expressions such as "right?" or "don't you agree?".

To reply to "Gobusata shite imasu," "Kochira koso (*Same here*)" is used. In casual conversations among friends, simply repeat "Hisashiburi!" or "Hisashiburi ne".

New Year's Celebration

The New Year is the most important time of the year in Japan. (*Just like Christmas in the west*).

At the end of the year:

Yoi otoshi o omukae kudasai. (*formal*)   I wish you will have a good new year.

Yoi otoshi o! (*casual*)

During New Year's days (*Jan. 1st to 3rd*), up to the middle of January:

Akemashite omedetou gozaimasu. (*formal*)   Happy New Year.

Akemashite omedetou. (*casual*)

"Akemasu" literally means "to open". "Kotoshi mo yoroshiku onegaishimasu (*I look forward to our continued relationship over this year*)" is often added after "Akemashite omedetou gozaimasu". To reply, "Kochira koso" is used.

Lesson 31

Talking on the phone

Even though you start understanding a language better, it is always difficult to talk on the phone in that language. You can't use gestures which help a lot most of the time. Also, you can't see the other person's facial expressions or reactions. You have to listen very carefully to what the other person says. Talking on the phone in Japanese might be especially harder, since there are some formal phrases customarily used in phone conversations. (*The Japanese normally talk very politely on the phone unless talking with a friend.*) Let's learn common expressions used on the phone. Don't be intimidated by phone calls. Practice makes perfect!

Phone Call in Japan

Most public phones (*koushuu denwa*) take coins (*at least a 10 yen coin*) and telephone cards. Only designated pay phones allow international calls (*kokusai denwa*). All calls are charged by the minute. Telephone cards can be purchased in almost all convenience stores, kiosks at train stations and vending machines. The cards are sold in 500 yen and 1000 yen units. Telephone cards can be customized. Some companies even use them as marketing tools. Some cards are very valuable, and cost a fortune. Many people collect telephone cards just like postage stamps are collected.

Telephone Number

A telephone number consists of the three parts, for example, *(03)* 2815-1311. The first part is the area code (*03 is Tokyo's*), and the second and last part are the user's number. Each number is usually read separately, linking the parts with the particle "no." In telephone numbers 0 is often pronounced as "zero," 4 as "yon" and 7 as "nana" to reduce confusion (*as 0, 4, 7 and 9 each have two different pronunciations*). If you are not familiar with Japanese numbers.

The most essential phrase is "moshi moshi." It is used by the caller when connected. It is also used when one can't hear the other person well, or to confirm if the other person is still on the line. Although some people say "moshi moshi" to answer the phone, "hai" is used more often in business.

If the other person speaks too fast, or you couldn't catch what he/she said, say "Yukkuri onegaishimasu (*Please speak slowly*)" or "Mou ichido onegaishimasu (*Please say it again*)." "Onegaishimasu" is a useful phrase when making a request.

At the Office

Business phone conversations are extremely polite. The mark * indicates the caller's phrases.

* Yamada-san (*o*) onegaishimasu.	Could I speak to Mr. Yamada?
Mousniwake arimasen ga, tadaima gaishutsu shiteorimasu.	I'm sorry, but he's not here at the moment.
Shou shou omachi kudasai.	Just a moment, please.
Shitsurei desu ga, dochira sama desu ka.	Who's calling, please?
* Naiji goro omodori desu ka.	Do you know what time he/she will be back?
Chotto wakarimasen.	I'm not sure.
Mousugu modoru to omoimasu.	He/she should be back soon.
Yuugata made modorimasen.	He/she won't be back till this evening.
* Nanika otsutae shimashou ka.	Can I take a message?
Onegaishimasu.	Yes, please.
Iie, kekkou desu.	No, it's O.K.
O-denwa kudasai to otsutae negaemasu ka.	Could you please ask him/her to call me?

Mata denwa shimasu to otsutae kudasai.	Could you please tell him/her I'll call back later?

To Somebody's Home

* **Tanaka-san no otaku desu ka.**	Is that Mrs. Tanaka's residence?
Hai, sou desu.	Yes, it is.
* **Ono desu ga, Yuki-san (wa) . irasshaimasu ka**	This is Ono. Is Yuki there?
* **Yabun osokuni sumimasen.**	I'm sorry for calling so late.
* **Dengon o onegaishimasu.**	Can I leave a message?
* **Mata atode denwa shimasu.**	I'll call back later.

How to Deal with Wrong Number

Iie chigaimasu.	No, you have called the wrong number.
* **Sumimasen. Machigaemashita.**	I'm sorry. I have misdialed.

Lesson 32

Visiting someone's place

Japanese seem to have many formal phrases for certain actions. When visiting your superior or somebody for the first time, these phrases will be helpful to express your gratitude. Here are some common expressions you are likely to use when visiting Japanese homes.

At the Door

Guest   **Konnichiwa.**

            Gomen kudasai.

Host   **Irasshai.**

            Irassaimase.

            Yoku irasshai mashita.

            Yookoso.

"Gomen kudasai" literally means, "Please forgive me for bothering you." It is often used when visiting someone's home. "Irassharu" is the honorific form (*keigo*) of the verb "kuru (*to come*)." All four expressions for a host mean "Welcome." "Irasshai" is less formal than other expressions. It should not be used when a guest is superior to a host.

When You Enter the Room

Host	**Doozo oagari kudasai.**	Please come in.
	Doozo ohairi kudasai.	
	Doozo kochira e.	This way, please.
Guest	**Ojama shimasu.**	Excuse me.
	Shitsurei shimasu.	

"Doozo" is very useful expression and means, "please." The Japanese use it quite often. "Doozo oagari kudasai" literally means, "Please come up." This is because Japanese houses usually have an elevated floor in the entrance (*genkan*) and step up to go into the house. Then, there is a well known tradition - taking off your shoes at the genkan. You might want to make sure your socks don't have any holes before visiting Japanese homes! A pair of slippers is often offered to wear in the house. When you enter a tatami (*a straw mat*) room, you should remove slippers.

"Ojama shimasu" literally means, "I'm going to get in your way" or " I will disturb you." It is used as a polite greeting when entering someone's home. "Shitsurei shimasu" literally means, "I'm going to be rude." This expression is used in various situations. When entering someone's house or room, it means "Excuse my interrupting." When leaving it is used as "Excuse my leaving" or "Good-bye."

When Giving a Gift

Tsumaranai mono desu ga ...   Here is something for you.

Kore doozo.   This is for you.

The Japanese customary bring a gift when visiting someone's home. The expression "Tsumaranai mono desu ga ..." is very Japanese. It literally means, "This is an trifling thing, but please accept it." It might sound strange to you. Why anyone brings such a thing as a gift? This is a humble expression. The humble form (*kenjougo*) is used when a speaker wants to lower his/her position. Therefore, this expression is often used to your superior, in spite of the true value of the gift. When giving a gift to your close friend or other informal occasions, "Kore doozo" will do it.

When Your Host Begins to Prepare Drinks or Food for You

Doozo okamainaku.   Please don't go to any trouble.

When Drinking or Eating

Host	**Doozo meshiagatte kudasai.**	Please help yourself.
Guest	**Itadakimasu.**	(*Before Eating*)
	Gochisousama deshita.	(*After Eating*)

"Meshiagaru" is the honorific form of the verb "taberu (*to eat*)." "Itadaku" is a humble form of the verb "morau (*to receive*)." However, "Itadakimasu" is a fixed expression used before eating or drinking. After eating "Gochisousama deshita" is used to express appreciation for the food. "Gochisou" literally means, "a feast." There is no religious significance of these phrases.

When Thinking about Leaving

Sorosoro shitsurei shimasu.   It is about time I should be leaving.

"Sorosoro" is a useful phrase for leaving. In informal situations, you could say "Sorosoro kaerimasu (*It's about time for me to go home*)," "Sorosoro kaerou ka (*Shall we go home soon?*)" or just "Ja sorosoro ... (*Well, it's about time ...*)" etc.

When Leaving Someone's Home

Ojama shimashita.   Excuse me.

"Ojama shimashita" literally means, "I got in the way." It is often used when leaving someone's home.

Lesson 33

Useful Japanese Phrases for Travellers

Do you plan to go for a trip to Japan? Learn some useful expressions before you go. Speaking the language of the country you are visiting makes the trip more fun!

Train

Tokyo eki wa doko desu ka.	Where is the Tokyo Station?
Kono densha wa ~ ni tomarimasu ka.	Does this train stop at ~?
Tsugi wa nani eki desu ka.	What is the next station?
Nanji ni demasu ka.	What time does it leave?
Nanji ni tsukimasu ka.	What time does it arrive?

Dono gurai kakarimasu ka.	How long does it take?
Oufuku no kippu o kudasai.	I would like to buy a return ticket.

Taxi

Osaka hoteru made onegaishimasu.	Please take me to the Hotel Osaka.
Osaka eki made ikura desu ka.	How much does it cost to go to the Osaka Station?
Massugu itte kudasai.	Please go straight.
Migi ni magatte kudasai.	Please turn right.
Hidari ni magatte kudasai.	Please turn left.

Bus

Basutei wa doko desu ka.	Where is the bus stop?
Kono basu wa Kyoto ni ikimasu ka.	Does this bus go to Kyoto?
Tsugi no basu wa nanji desu ka.	What time is the next bus?

Car

Doko de kuruma o kariru koto ga dekimasu ka.	Where can I rent a car?
Ichinichi ikura desu ka.	How much is it

daily?

Mantan ni shite kudasai. Please fill the tank.

Koko ni kuruma o tomete mo ii desu ka. Can I park here?

Air

Osaka iki no bin wa arimasu ka. Is there a flight to Osaka?

Nanji ni chekku-in shitara ii desu ka. What time should I check in?

Shinkoku suru mono wa arimasen. I have nothing to declare.

Shinkoku suru mono ga arimasu. I have something to declare.

Shigoto de isshuukan taizai shimasu. I am going to stay here for a week on business.

Others

Toire wa doko desu ka. Where is the washroom?

~ ni wa dou ikeba ii desu ka. How do I get to ~?

Koko kara chikai desu ka. Is it near here?

Aruite ikemasu ka. Can I walk there?

Lesson 34

Expressing health problems

    Here are some expressions to describe physical conditions. Pain is usually described using the adjective "itai (*painful, sore*)".

atama ga itai	to have a headache
ha ga itai	to have a toothache
nodo ga itai	to have a sore throat
onaka ga itai	to have a stomachache
seki ga deru	to have a cough
hana ga deru	to have a runny nose
netsu ga aru	to have a fever
samuke ga suru	to have a chill
karada ga darui	to feel a lack of energy
shokuyoku ga nai	to have no appetite
memai ga suru	to feel dizzy
kaze o hiku	to catch a cold

When describing your conditions to a doctor, "~n desu" is often added at the end of the sentence. It has an explanatory function. To express "I have a cold," "kaze o hikimashita" or "kaze o hiiteimasu" is used.

Atama ga itai n desu.   I have a headache.

Netsu ga aru n desu.   I have a fever.

Here is how to express degrees of pain.

totemo itai   very painful

sukoshi itai   a little bit painful

Onomatopoeic expressions are also used to express degrees of pain. "Gan gan" or "zuki zuki" is used to describe headaches. "Zuki zuki" or "shiku shiku" is used for toothaches and "kiri kiri" or "shiku shiku" for stomachaches.

gan gan   pounding headache

zuki zuki   throbbing pain

shiku shiku   dull pain

kiri kiri   sharp continuous pain

hiri hiri   burning pain

chiku chiku   prickly pain

Lesson 35

Family

Standard family nouns

Japanese family nouns are categorized in two groups: standard family nouns and calling family nouns. The latter is used to call your family without using their name, like the English words *dad* and *mom*. Standard family nouns are never used to call them in your family.

Kana:

Accent:	L	H'
Romanization:	o	ya
Meaning:	parent	

Note: Another word H'L "fubo", which means *father and mother*, is also commonly used in formal situations.

Kana:

Accent:	H'	L
Romanization:	chi	chi
Meaning:	father	

Note: The word LHHH "chichioya" is also commonly used for *father*, even though it is linguistically redundant.

Kana:

Accent:	H'	L
Romanization:	ha	ha
Meaning:	mother	

Note: The word LHHH "hahaoya" is also commonly used for *mother*.

Kana:

Accent:	H'	L
Romanization:	a	ni
Meaning:	elder brother	

Note: Japanese distinguishes elder brothers and younger brothers. The word H'LLL "kyôdai" means *brothers and sisters* and it is sometimes useful, but using it for a specific brother/sister is as strange as using the English word *sibling* for him/her. It depends on language what information you have to give when you talk about a sibling. You have to clarify his/her sex and age compared to you in Japanese, while in English you don't have to tell his/her age. You might be interested to know that in Indonesian you have to clarify only his/her age, so the Indonesian word for *elder brother* also means *elder sister*.

Kana:

Accent:	L	H
Romanization:	a	ne
Meaning:	elder sister	

Kana:

Accent:	L		H	H	H'
Romanization:	o		tô	to	

Meaning: younger brother

Kana:

Accent:	L		H	H	H'
Romanization:	i		mô	to	

Meaning: younger sister

Kana:

Accent:	H'	L
Romanization:	so	fu

Meaning: grandfather

Kana:

Accent:	H'	L
Romanization:	so	bo

Meaning: grandmother

Note: The word LH'L "sofubo" means *grandfather and grandmother*.

Kana:

Accent:	L
Romanization:	ko

Meaning: child

Note: Another word LHH "kodomo" is also commonly used for *child*, but it often means all minors, not only your sons and daughters.

Kana:			
Accent:	L	H	H
Romanization:	mu	su	ko
Meaning:	son		

Kana:			
Accent:	L	H	H'
Romanization:	mu	su	me
Meaning:	daughter		

Kana:		
Accent:	L	H'
Romanization:	ma	go
Meaning:	grandchild	

Note: If you want to distinguish grandsons and grand-daughters, you can use LHH'LL "magomusuko" (*grand-son*) and LHH'LL "magomusume" (*grand daughter*), but simply saying is commoner.

Kana:		
Accent:	L	H
Romanization:	o	ji
Meaning:	uncle	

Kana:		
Accent:	L	H
Romanization:	o	ba
Meaning:	aunt	

Kana:			
Accent:	H'	L	L

Romanization:	i	to	ko
Meaning:	cousin		
Kana:			
Accent:	L	H	

Romanization:	o	i
Meaning:	nephew	
Kana:		
Accent:	L	H

Romanization:	me	i
Meaning:	niece	

Calling family nouns

The following words are used to call elder members of your family, like *dad* and *mom*. It is also good to use them to refer to other people's families, but using them to talk about your own family in formal situations sounds childish. Use given names to call younger members of your family.

Kana:					
Accent:	L	H'	L	L	L
Romanization:	o	tô	sa	n	
Meaning:	dad				

Note: The first "o" is a common politeness prefix for nouns, and removing it sounds you are matured. The last "san" is the same as the Japanese equivalent of Mr. and Ms., but it's a part of the word and you can't remove it.

Kana:

Accent: L   H'   L   L

Romanization: o   kâ   sa   n

Meaning: mom

Kana:

Accent: L   H'   L   L   L

Romanization: o   nî   sa   n

Meaning: elder brother (calling name)

Note: Children prefer the word LH'LLL "onîchan". The last "chan" is a childlike version of.

Kana:

Accent: L   H'   L   L   L

Romanization: o   nê   sa   n

Meaning: elder sister (calling name)

Note: Children prefer the word LH'LLL "onêchan".

Kana:

Accent: L   H'   L   L   L

Romanization: o   jî   cha   n

Meaning: grandpa

Note: The word LH'LLL "ojîsan" is often used for old men in general, not necessarily your grandfather.

Kana:

Accent: L   H'   L   L   L

Romanization: o   bâ   cha   n

Meaning: grandma

Note: The word LH'LLL "obâsan" is often used for old women in general, not necessarily your grandmother.

Kana:				
Accent:	L	H	H	H
Romanization:	o	ji	sa	n
Meaning:	uncle (calling name)			

Note: This word is also used for general middle-age men.

Kana:				
Accent:	L	H	H	H
Romanization:	o	ba	sa	n
Meaning:	aunt (calling name)			

Note: This word is also used for general middle-age women.

The interesting point of the calling family nouns is that the viewpoint is usually fixed on the youngest member of the family. For example, it is not uncommon at all for a man with a kid to call his wife "okâsan" and for his wife to call her husband "otôsan", because their word usage is based on their kid's viewpoint. If they live with his or her parents, they would call their father "ojîchan" and their mother "obâchan".